Hide-and-Seek

Pete, Jem and Belle play hide-and-seek. Pete has a very good hiding spot – will Jem and Belle ever find him?

Targeting Subject-Verb-Object sentences and prepositions, this book provides repeated examples of early developing syntax and morphology which will engage and excite the reader while building pre-literacy skills and making learning fun. It also exposes the reader to multiple models of the target grammar form.

Perfect for a speech and language therapy session, this book is an ideal starting point for targeting client goals and can also be enjoyed at school or at home to reinforce what has been taught in the therapy session.

Jessica Habib studied speech pathology at the University of Sydney, graduating in 2012. She has since worked with children in indigenous health, community, private, not-for-profit and education settings in both Australia and the UK. Jessica loves the privilege she has of seeing children thrive as they are guided to build and strengthen their communication skills.

Carina Ward is an illustrator based in the Blue Mountains, Australia. She works with watercolour and ink to create beautiful, bright images and likes to add a touch of humour to her work. Carina loves the way pictures tell stories and open up imaginary worlds.

T0141299

What's in the pack?

Hide-and-Seek

A *Grammar Tales* Book to Support Grammar and Language Development in Children

Jessica Habib

Illustrated by Carina Ward

Routledge
Taylor & Francis Group

LONDON AND NEW YORK

Cover image: Carina Ward

First published 2023
by Routledge
4 Park Square, Milton Park, Abingdon, Oxon OX14 4RN

and by Routledge
605 Third Avenue, New York, NY 10158

Routledge is an imprint of the Taylor & Francis Group, an informa business

© 2023 Jessica Habib and Carina Ward

The right of Jessica Habib to be identified as author of this work and Carina Ward to be identified as illustrator of this work has been asserted in accordance with sections 77 and 78 of the Copyright, Designs and Patents Act 1988.

All rights reserved. No part of this book may be reprinted or reproduced or utilised in any form or by any electronic, mechanical, or other means, now known or hereafter invented, including photocopying and recording, or in any information storage or retrieval system, without permission in writing from the publishers.

Trademark notice: Product or corporate names may be trademarks or registered trademarks, and are used only for identification and explanation without intent to infringe.

British Library Cataloguing-in-Publication Data
A catalogue record for this book is available from the British Library

Library of Congress Cataloging-in-Publication Data
A catalog record for this book has been requested

ISBN: 978-1-032-27432-4 (pbk)
ISBN: 978-1-003-29273-9 (ebk)

DOI: 10.4324/9781003292739

Typeset in Calibri
by Apex CoVantage, LLC

Hide-and-Seek

Jem counts to ten.

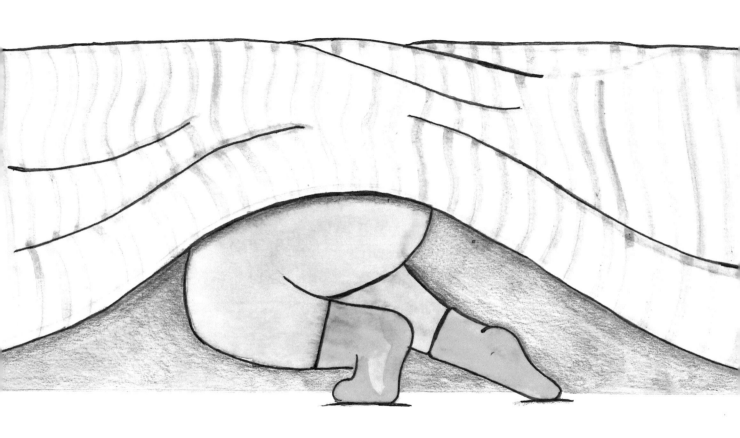

Pete hides under the bed.

Belle hides in the toybox.

em looks out
he front.

She looks in the bath.

She looks under
the rug.

She looks on
the bookshelf.

6

Jem finds Belle!

Jem and Belle look for Pete.

Jem looks in the cupboard.

Belle crawls out of the cupboard.

Jem looks on the windowsill.
Belle looks under the blanket.

Belle looks on the bed.

She climbs off the bed.

Jem checks on the trampoline.
Belle bounces off the trampoline.

Where is Pete?

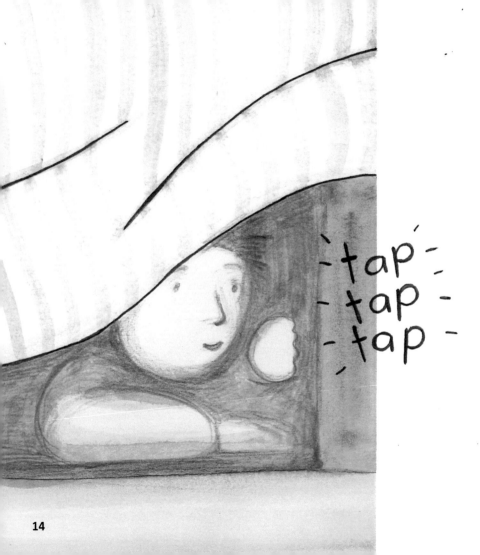

15

They find Pete under the bed!

AuQ1

Pete counts to ten.

Where is Jem?

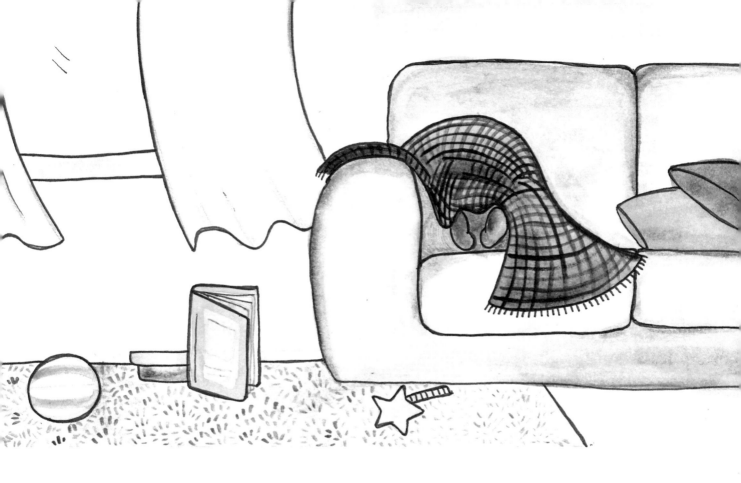

Where is Belle?